PRECONSCIOUS

MARKETING

Designing brands that can deeply connect with customers

Ramanathan J

PRECONSCIOUS MARKETING

Cover designed by Ramanathan J

Contents

INTRODUCTION

I like to browse through the online Steam store frequently in order to check out the new computer games that are available for purchase. Steam store is an online marketplace where any game developer can make any game available to the audience for purchase and download. Game developers can range from one-man team, who would have probably designed, developed and tested an entire game from his garage to a complete studio that can rival any Hollywood production crew.

Once a game is available on the Steam store, it is open for rigorous scrutiny and relentless feedback from the gaming community. The gaming community is quick and often accurate to judge a game within just few hours after a studio releases a title. This is because Steam store subscribers can purchase a game, play it for two hours and if in case they do not like the product, they can ask for a full refund within the two hours of purchase.

Now some games on this store are truly remarkable. These titles are developed by legions of professionals from big developer studios and have the production values of a Hollywood blockbuster movie. Many of these games make good money from sales and obtain good returns on their development and marketing budgets. Some games do not impress the target audience a lot and hence as a result, these games generate average or below average sales. However, occasionally, a relatively small or unknown game developer studio releases a product that literally leaves the gaming community spellbound. I recently stumbled upon one such masterpiece of a game in the Steam store when I was casually browsing for new titles.

Factorio – The digital drug

Computer games can focus on any specific genre thereby identifying its niche audience. For example, some games are action oriented while others may focus on sports such as soccer or basketball. Factorio provided gameplay experience focused on automation, strategy and resource management. When I saw the trailer for the Factorio game for the first time, I was not too impressed by the low-resolution graphics and few gameplay videos of supply chains. I decided to skip reading the reviews and I chose to play the game anyway.

You play the role of a lone explorer in Factorio. You are stuck in an alien planet and the objective of you as a player in this game is to escape this alien planet by building a rocket. Building a rocket requires materials as well as resources. You as a player in this game can build systems, automate resource collection and optimize various supply chains to produce the materials that are required to build the rocket.

I downloaded Factorio and started to play this game at around 9 AM. The game interface was simple and intuitive. Controls were mostly based on drag and drop as well as on few keys. My player character in the game started to mine few blocks of coal, iron and copper. This was obviously a very inefficient way to extract resources and hence I had to improvise upon my strategy. Soon, I set up a power generator that used coal as a resource. I used the electricity from this generator to extract more coal. This excess coal would then be supplied to additional power generators that would generate more electricity.

Then I automated the extraction of other resources such as iron and copper. Every minute I played the game, I discovered an objective that was challenging but was achievable by applying some ingenuity. The objectives also became more complex as I spent more time playing the game. For example, I had to combine iron and copper resources to manufacture steel plates and later I had to extract crude oil and use it as an additional ingredient in the manufacturing process. There was an additional challenge of maintaining the production efficiency in order to ensure that one supply chain does not end up waiting for resources from some other production line.

When I stopped playing Factorio for the day, I looked at the clock and I discovered that it was 2 PM. I played Factorio for 5 hours non-stop from 9 AM and I was never aware about the same while I was engrossed trying to optimize my manufacturing chains in the game.

I then looked back into the Steam store to read reviews for Factorio. This game had a large number of 'Overwhelmingly Positive' rating on Steam, a rare feat for any game developer. Many players mentioned in their reviews that they started to play the game in the evening and then when they stopped playing it, they realized that it was early in the morning. These players preferred to skip dinner and sleep and were instead more keen to play the game in order to solve the next challenging yet attainable task. Several players said that they were not concerned by their needs to attend to hunger, thirst or rest and were instead more bothered about progressing further towards the next goal in Factorio.

Thus, many players aptly labelled this game as a digital drug or a narcotic. If you are thinking of discovering more about this game or if you are planning to try this game, I would urge you to stay away. If in case you go ahead and play this game anyhow, it is highly possible that you may sit in front of your computer for 12 hours straight playing this game and yet you would still feel that you have only spent an hour or two. The creators of Factorio have definitely developed a work of art that has managed to attract the attention of many consumers for a long period.

Implications for marketing and branding – From Factorio

We live in an attention-deprived world. We shuffle through cable TV channels in a matter of minutes. We can browse through a website for few seconds before we switch to another internet browser tab. Finally, we will respond to a chat on WhatsApp and then look at a shopping app before selecting a new song on the playlist in our smartphones in few moments. Consumer attention is a precious commodity and any brand, product or service that can win over this attention for few key moments will rule the markets. Companies allocate huge sums of money as marketing budgets, hire perceptive creative agencies and analyse enormous data in order to devise the right strategy to capture the elusive attention of their customers.

When I played Factorio, hours literally passed as minutes. I checked the online reviews and many other players also felt that they skipped hours. Many players were also unable to stop thinking about the game and its objectives long after they shut down their computers.

From a marketing or branding perspective, Factorio has achieved an enormous feat. This game captured the attention of many players for hours at a stretch. Any brand or product that can achieve even a fraction of what Factorio managed to accomplish will be able to dominate the market over other competitors. This game as a concept contains the perfect cocktail of idea, aesthetic and design that has been able to tap into some mysterious and ancient circuit inside a consumer's mind, which constantly craves for excitement, novelty, feedback and reward.

I was curious to understand more about how a product, idea or concept can become enthralling enough to obtain and sustain the attention or focus of a target audience. I wanted to explore how a brand can ensure favourable action from a consumer subsequently, which would be to purchase the product and to stay committed to the brand. To summarize, I was keen to explore the Factorio effect. I wanted to understand how companies could achieve a similar result for their brands, products or services. What can companies do to convince the inherent value of their brands to the most fascinating piece of biological wonder present with any consumer –

the human brain?

THE HUMAN BRAIN- A MARVELLOUS MACHINE

The brain is one part of the human anatomy that inspires both awe and amazement. If a primitive human being has managed to survive the harsh environment of forests and has been able to form civilizations and societies, then the brain must take a great credit for this accomplishment. Human beings have constantly relied on the efficiency and decision making ability of their brains to react and to adapt to the external environment.

Human brain comprises of a dense network that links nearly 100 Billion neurons through 100 Trillion synapses or connections. Neurons are functional cells and a fundamental unit of the nervous system. Neurons transmit and receive nerve impulses. Synapse represents a junction between two neurons. A small gap exists at the synapse. Nerve impulses cross the synapse with the help of neurotransmitters.

An average human brain takes up approximately 3 percent of total body weight but consumes nearly 20 percent of total blood and oxygen produced in a human being. This indicates the extent of activities and functions for which the human brain is responsible. This fascinating super computer like organ processes information, evaluates options, inspires new ideas and motivates humans to perform certain actions.

Functions of nervous system

Brain and the associated nervous systems are responsible for the smooth functioning and survival of any human being. The nervous system can be classified into two key regions namely the central nervous system (CNS) and the peripheral nervous system (PNS). The CNS comprises of brain and the spinal cord whereas the PNS comprises of nerves that originate from the spinal cord and branch off to various parts of the human body.

The basic functions of the nervous system are to receive information about the surrounding environment and to respond based on this information. The nervous system uses sensation or sensory functions to gather information about the external environment. The nervous system responds to this information using motor functions. Another key function of the nervous system is to associate input with other sensations, memories, emotions or learning. Some regions of the nervous system are involved in integrating or associating sensations with other cognitive inputs such as memories or emotions before producing a response.

The nervous system receives information about the external environment using senses. The five major senses utilized by the nervous system to gather inputs include taste, smell, touch, sight and hearing. The nervous system notes an event or a change in the external environment by detecting stimuli for the various senses.

The stimuli for various senses are as follows:

1. For taste and smell – certain chemical substances

2. For sight – light

3. For touch – physical or mechanical stimuli that interact with skin

4. For hearing – perception of sound

We have a conscious perception or awareness of all the information that we gather using our senses from the outside world.

The nervous system produces a response based on the information gathered from the sensory functions. A response could be conscious or voluntary in nature such as moving the hand away from a hot utensil. A response can also be unconscious or involuntary in nature. For e.g. Contraction of muscles or activation of sweat glands are involuntary responses. Information generated from various stimuli is often associated with other stimuli, memories or emotions to produce an integrated response.

Some of the voluntary motor responses are reflexive in nature. Hence, we need not think consciously before performing such responses. For example, we reflexively move our hand away when we touch a hot glass of water. We did not think or evaluate consciously whether the glass of water is hot enough to hold or should we move our hand away. Reflexive motor response enables us to act in a flight or fight mode and has provided us with an evolutionary advantage while surviving in a tough external environment.

Other motor responses become automatic over a period after we learn these motor skills. For e.g. when we drive a car for the first time, we need to apply conscious thought to perform various activities such as applying brakes, pressing on accelerator, adjusting the steering wheel, watching the fuel gauge and observing the speedometer. However, when we practise to drive the car over a period, we learn to perform these skills automatically without applying enough conscious thought. Learned motor responses enable us to save time and to perform complex tasks with great precision. Like reflexive motor response, learned motor responses have also provided us with an evolutionary advantage because we are able to build new skills and apply them for our benefit in various scenarios.

Learned motor responses play a significant role for customers who are loyal to a particular brand when they need a product or service. For e.g. you may automatically choose a brand of potato chips when you visit a supermarket. Similarly, you may not think twice when you select a specific airline for your next business trip. You might have similar preferences for your toothpaste, soap or restaurant. Customer loyalty relies on learned motor responses that expects and prefers a certain set of experiences from a brand.

System defaults for our brains

We have now observed the enormity of tasks and responsibilities that our brain has to fulfil in order to keep us functioning well. Our brain takes inputs from the senses, analyses the data to decide upon the best response and handles the functioning of our internal organs simultaneously. Even when we are asleep, our brain continues to manage our internal systems. The human brain is never overwhelmed at the prospect of analysing a non-stop stream of sensory data and deciding upon the appropriate response. The human brain continues to operate at optimum levels because it relies on four fundamental principles for its functioning. These fundamental principles for human brain are similar to default settings for an operating system on a computer.

Energy conservative: Our brain consumes a disproportionate share of the total energy or calories produced in a human being. However, our brain is very conservative when it comes to expending energy for processing any information or for deciding a course of action.

We will face inaction if our brain were to pay equal amount of attention to every sensory input that it constantly receives from the five senses. As a result, our brain prioritizes speed over efficiency. Our brain relies on shortcuts such as learned motor skills or muscle memory to decide upon the ideal response for many sensory inputs that we encounter frequently. Hence, we do not have to spend our precious cognitive resources such as attention or conscious decision making for every little task that we face.

For e.g. we stop our car when we see a red signal without consciously thinking about the same. Our mind processes the meaning of red signal and the response in an automatic manner. Similarly, when we learn to drive a car for the first time, we apply a great degree of conscious thought and action to our every single step. However, as we continue to practise the various steps required for driving a car, we build muscle memory for the skill. Our ability to build skills and expertise enables us to conserve our cognitive faculties such as attention for critical tasks.

Novelty Seeking: If our brain seeks to conserve energy and attention for critical tasks or sensory inputs, then the obvious question is how does our brain determine which sensory input is worth paying attention to. How does our brain determine which sensory input needs our conscious intervention and which ones will be processed by our learned motor responses?

The answer is novelty. Our brain actively scans the environment for anything out of ordinary using our sensory organs. If we sense that anything is out of place or does not belong to that location, our attention is naturally drawn to that object. This tendency of our brain to pay attention to novel objects in the surrounding environment has an evolutionary reason as well. Cave dwelling primitive man had to pay attention to novel objects in the external environment for his survival. If a predator were to lurk behind the bushes, the primitive man had to react quickly in order to escape on time. Our brain is hard wired to seek novelty in our immediate surroundings. As a result, brands or products seek to infuse novelty in their packaging or marketing communication materials in order to draw the attention of consumers.

Familiarity Inclination: Although we do pay attention to the novel items in our surroundings, we are wary or suspicious of these unique objects. This behaviour also has an evolutionary background as well. For e.g. if our cave dwelling man spotted a predator in the woods, he would have initially paid attention to it. However, he would then rightly perceive the predator to be dangerous. Subsequently, our cave dweller would flee from the spot to escape from the predator.

Thus, although our brain pays attention to unique objects in our surroundings, it quickly becomes suspicious of these unique items. However, our brain has an inclination for familiar objects and environments. Familiarity indicates security for our brain. Human beings are also social animals. They interact with other fellow human beings to form families, tribes and societies. Familiarity indicates home, friends and family for a human being. Our brain feels secure and can let its guard down in a familiar environment. As a result, our brain prefers familiarity in surrounding environment and objects.

Companies must be cautious when they seek to position their products or brands as too unique or novel as compared to the rest of the market. Customers might initially pay attention to such brands. However, these customers would eventually prefer familiar products.

Simplicity Bias: As we observed earlier, human brain prefers to conserve energy and cognitive faculties for critical tasks. When our brain faces a challenging task, it has to dedicate a substantial amount of attention and willpower to complete the activity. As a result, our brain seeks simplicity while processing any sensory input.

This preference for simplicity is clearly visible when we observe consumer preferences for electronic appliances or technology products. Earlier, people could use computers only by typing commands for performing various operations. As a result, computer sales were not that widespread in the market. However, user adoption for computers increased dramatically when companies introduced graphical user interface or GUI technology. Users can now operate computers by placing the cursor and clicking various icons on the screen with a mouse. Simplicity of use proved crucial in transforming the personal computer industry.

We can similarly attribute the enormous success of Microsoft Excel spreadsheet software to the extremely simple user interface and functionality of the product. Users can work with Excel in any way that they want. The product also provides multiple functions or features that are elegantly located in menu bars, tool bars or in the background as a formula or a function. As a result, users get a product that is clutter free and simple to use.

Companies must emphasize on elegance and simplicity while positioning their products or brands. A consumer can easily process a clutter free brand that provides simplicity of options and features.

Associative learning or priming

Priming is an important process that a human brain utilizes in order to analyse the incoming sensory data and to determine the ideal response. Priming prepares the ground for our brain to process the sensory inputs in a certain context. Priming also establishes a cause and effect type of link between different various thoughts, sensations and responses. Thus, priming is a type of cognitive processing short cut that enables our brain to prioritize speed over efficiency.

Priming prepares the internal mechanisms in human beings for subsequent steps or actions. Priming occurs instantly within human beings without any need for conscious intervention or effort. Hence, priming links one idea to other related ideas that in turn sets the stage for other associated behaviour and actions.

External stimuli such as visual or auditory triggers as well as internal thoughts or ideas can trigger priming in human beings. One possible reason for this phenomenon could be the ability of human beings to imagine in a vivid manner. Hence, even a thought or an idea that a human being imagines in detail is equivalent to observing a visual stimuli.

The key point to note here is that the thoughts or ideas related to one topic could prime the subject for behaviour or action in a completely different context. For e.g. in one study, researchers asked subjects to solve crossword puzzle that contained words related to aging. These subjects later demonstrated a slow walking pace after completing the task.

Priming may also have an evolutionary origin that could have helped primitive human beings to survive in a tough environment. For e.g. the primitive cave dweller would have looked at the rough shape of a four-legged predator hiding in the bushes waiting to ambush its next prey. The visual trigger of a four-legged wild animal would have been sufficient to trigger the ideas of danger and run in the cave dweller. Thus, the visual trigger of a predator primed our primitive cave dweller to get alarmed and to escape.

Priming also prepares our internal systems for subsequent actions. For e.g. we salivate automatically when we observe a delicious food. However, we also feel the need to eat when we look at a high-resolution picture of a delicacy or when we read about the ingredients and rich texture of a pizza. This is because the human brain cannot differentiate between richly imagined detail and reality. We can trigger human imagination with a high-resolution picture or even a detailed text.

Priming is the most crucial objective of any advertisement or visual display. Companies seek to prime consumers towards purchasing the target brand or product through advertisements. Some advertisements or marketing communication materials emphasize on highlighting the product features or benefits. These features are information that a consumer has to process before he can assign a meaning to any brand. Some advertisements focus on displaying rich imagery of a product along with the brand so that the customer may link the two ideas automatically through priming. Hence, if a consumer sees a high-resolution poster of pizza along with the logo of Pizza Hut, he is primed to crave for pizza. The consumer is also primed towards associating Pizza Hut brand with delicious pizzas. Even when a consumer walks by a bakery that is preparing cakes, the aroma of freshly baked cakes can prime him towards craving for cake.

Priming can also be immensely beneficial for companies that want to induce a certain state of mind among its target consumers. For e.g. a holiday resort can include words such as relax, calm and serene as a part of the description in its brochure and print advertisement in order to induce a state of relaxation among consumers who will read the advertisement. As a result, consumers will be primed towards associating the holiday resort with the qualities of relaxation and serenity. Similarly, an underdog brand can take on bigger competition by priming the customers for taking a logical or questioning stance towards competing brands.

For e.g. a new restaurant can make consumers question the established or dominant competition by including phrases on the lines of "Are you really getting good service and quality food in restaurants today? Think carefully and answer" in its advertisements. This text will prime consumers to adopt a critical or analytical stance towards the competing brands. Consumers will soon begin to find flaws among the competitors. A separate advertisement campaign can prime the customers to associate the new restaurant brand with desirable ideas such as great food and service.

Unconscious, subconscious or preconscious?

Numerous books and articles over the years have divided the human mind into conscious and subconscious layers. Conscious mind is broadly defined to have the ability to analyse and consciously process any information before determining a possible response in the form of behaviour, decision or action. Subconscious mind is supposed to be capable of autonomous functioning and hence does not require any conscious supervision.

Some books refer to the subconscious mind as unconscious mind. I would rather prefer to call subconscious layer of mind as preconscious mind. I think that the term preconscious indicates a layer of mind that precedes the conscious intervention or analysis.

If we compare a human being to a super tanker ship, then the conscious mind is the captain's deck and the preconscious mind is the massive engine. Just like the ship captain who relies on the navigation system within the deck to make sense of the directions and the surrounding environment, human beings rely on the conscious mind to analyse the incoming sensory data. Human beings also use conscious mind to think about possibilities and to plan for various objectives.

However, preconscious mind is responsible for regulating the internal systems of a human being. Preconscious mind works independently for 24 hours in a day to ensure that our internal organs are functioning properly. Like the engine in a super tanker, preconscious mind powers the human being to function at an optimum level. Preconscious mind operates outside the purview or supervision of the conscious mind. Yet, preconscious mind plays a key role in shaping the behaviour and actions of any human being. Thoughts that a human being consistently repeats over a period are hardwired as beliefs in a human being. Similarly, humans form habits after performing an action repeatedly. Preconscious mind eventually takes control over beliefs and habits in order to enable human beings to perform the related tasks in an automated manner. This enables the brain to delegate many tasks to the preconscious mind while conserving the cognitive faculties for processing novel inputs.

For example, what do you do when you run out of toothpaste? You would most likely pick up your preferred brand of toothpaste the next time when you go to the local supermarket without thinking much about it.

Do you remember when did you pick up your current brand of toothpaste for the first time? Chances are that you would have tried a specific brand of toothpaste for the first and then you would have liked the taste or the flavour of the brand. You would have then decided that you should purchase the toothpaste again for a few times and as a result, this brand of toothpaste would have become your preferred and default choice.

You may have similar preferences for other daily items such as soap, detergent, cookies, beverages or coffee powder. Many brand selections of consumers are hardwired preferences that enable quick decision making and help to conserve the cognitive resources. However, when you go to a new restaurant for the first time, you consciously look into the menu, check the prices and think about what you want to eat before placing the order.

You do not have encoded choices or preferences for dishes when you enter into a new restaurant for the first time. As a result, you rely on your conscious mind to evaluate and process various information before you decide on what you want to eat.

Brands that can induce individuals to engage in repeated buying actions will eventually become the preferred choice for consumers. Preferred brands are like impregnable fortresses in consumers' minds. When a consumer frequently uses a particular product or service, he strongly prefers a brand choice. For e.g. we brush daily using a specific brand of toothpaste. As a result, we are primed to correlate the need to brush daily with the need for a toothpaste and a specific brand as a choice for this toothpaste.

Emotions – the gateway to preconscious mind

Do you remember the last time when you saw a good movie? What are the aspects related to the movie that you could recall now? Chances are that you can recollect the overall plot of the movie. Perhaps you can also recall how you felt after watching this movie. Maybe you would have felt inspired or elated if you had watched a comedy. Alternatively, you would have felt thrill and excitement if you had watched an action adventure. Movies depend on gripping plots or scripts to trigger certain emotions among the audience. Movies that can generate the desired emotions among target audience become great success in the box office. Consumers evaluate not only movies but also other products and services based on the emotions that the brands create within them.

For e.g. If a consumer visits a restaurant and he is served a dish that is not prepared as per the expectations, then the consumer will feel cheated and disgusted after the experience. These emotions of betrayal and disgust will henceforth guide the consumer when he has to visit a restaurant in the future.

Consumers evaluate brands through the emotional outcomes that finally result from using the product or service related to the brand. Any brand that is able to trigger the desired emotions among its target consumers is a success. Customers will favourably evaluate a hotel that is able to create the emotions of friendliness, comfort and care among its guests through its service. However, customers will emphasize more on any negative emotions as compared to any positive emotions resulting from the brand.

Hence, if the hotel provides comfortable rooms to its guests but if the establishment employs discourteous staff, then these guests will evaluate the hotel brand based on unfriendly service. Negative emotional outcomes will overshadow or dominate the final evaluation of any brand among customers.

Thus, it is crucial for companies to understand the various touchpoints or interactions that customers have with any brand. Subsequently, companies can determine the emotional outcomes that a brand creates at each of these touchpoints or interactions. Finally, organizations can plan to handle any negative emotional outcomes created during any individual interaction in order to improve the overall customer evaluation of the brand. Thus, breaking down the overall brand experience into discrete stages is a key part of the analysis.

Companies can use customer journey maps and observational interviews to map the emotional outcomes to the various touchpoints while interacting with a brand. Companies can also alter environmental settings to observe their impact on the emotional outcome of a brand during individual interactions. For e.g. you can check staff friendliness with hotel guests during day, night, weekend, weekdays, holidays, summer or winter seasons. Environmental variables can also affect the emotional outcomes of customers with a brand at various touchpoints.

Emotion is a type of shortcut that a human brain uses to evaluate any scenario and to determine the best response. Our brain defines brands through experiences. Our brain also assigns meaning to experiences through the eventual emotions that are created after interacting with a brand.

The customer will either prefer or reject a brand based on the intensity of the various individual emotional outcomes that are created from the total experience.

Hence, if a restaurant provides great food but has unfriendly staff, the customers will soon evaluate the brand from the hostile environment rather than the delicious food.

We observed earlier that the autonomous nervous system manages the internal systems or the physiology of any human being by regulating the responses for various organs. From a human mind perspective, we also saw that the preconscious layer independently regulates the physiology of a human being without the need for any conscious intervention. However, emotions also affect the physiology of any human being. Emotional outcomes can create lasting impression on any individual by overriding conscious evaluation and analysis.

Our preconscious mind regulates the creation of perspiration from the respective glands in order to cool our body temperature. However, we also perspire when we are anxious. Thus, an emotional state of anxiety is also causing a change in the physiology or internal systems. This phenomenon indicates that our preconscious mind is open to emotional inputs. Our preconscious mind takes cues from the emotional outcomes for various experiences in order to determine whether to prefer or to avoid such experiences in the future. These responses transform into learned motor skills that would guide a consumer either to prefer or to avoid a brand.

What is one of the most proven technique to manage the emotions felt by any consumer towards a brand? The answer lies in exploring the enormous power of storytelling in order to understand how stories can transform brands.

THE POWER OF STORYTELLING

Do you remember the last time when you experienced a great story? Maybe you watched a blockbuster movie in a nearby multiplex or perhaps you heard a funny incident from your friend. Can you recall your state of mind when you were watching the movie or when you were listening to your friend who was narrating the amusing tale?

It is possible that you would have been completely immersed in the scene described in the movie or tale. You would have empathized with your favourite character. Your mind would have been transported to the environment described in the movie or the story. A compelling story combined with the power of imagination can enthral any individual.

Stories are not just one of the ways to entertain people. Storytelling have an evolutionary origin as well. The cave dwelling primitive man did not stay alone for long. The primitive man started family and joined forces with other cave dwellers to establish a tribe. It was necessary to share learning and experience among fellow tribe members and family.

Storytelling became one of the most crucial methods of sharing wisdom. Folk tales and legends were necessary to ensure that members of the tribe learn the strategies for survival in a tough environment. Some regions in India continue to transmit learning to the next generations in a verbal form through stories. Stories can provide significant meaning to any context, person, location or object. A story can turn a list of facts into an interesting narrative or plot.

The greatest advantage of an interesting story is that it leaves a lasting impression in the minds of a listener. If I ask you the plot of your all-time favourite movie, you will be able to recall the key elements of story effortlessly.

Stories can be an effective way for organizations to leave an enduring footprint about their brands in the minds of customers. Human beings love good stories and this is evident by the billions of dollars that production studios in Hollywood earn every year. A great story could differentiate between an outstanding and average brand in the market.

Founder's legend

What is the first thought that comes to your mind when you listen or read the words "Virgin Atlantic"? You would have most likely thought of Sir Richard Branson, the stylish founder of the Virgin Group. You would have read a number of articles or you would have watched countless documentaries and news footage about Sir Branson. You would also be aware about various trivia related to Sir Branson such as how he dropped out of school as a teenager or how he has crossed the Atlantic in a hot air balloon. The iconic entrepreneur is a brand in himself.

Similarly, what comes to your mind when you look at the logo for the Apple Company? You would have almost immediately thought of Steve Jobs. As in case of Sir Richard Branson, you would have read numerous articles and you would have viewed many news footages and documentaries that talked about Steve Jobs. You would be most likely aware of the various interesting facts about the iconic founder of Apple such as how Steve Jobs dropped out of college, how he took lessons in calligraphy or how he wandered across Northern India as a part of his spiritual quest.

In case of both Virgin Atlantic and Apple, stories of their founders dominate the company or the brand itself. In fact, customers often associate the qualities of the founders to the brand. Customers will describe the

Virgin Atlantic brand as flamboyant or dynamic. Similarly, many customers will describe Apple brand as creative or innovative. Customers expect brands to inherit the characteristics of founders just like children who would share at least some traits from their parents. Such brands can build on the charisma and the personality of their founders in order to carve out a distinct space in the minds of the customers.

Now you may debate that Steve Jobs revolutionized the technology space with his innovative products and as a result, the media created an icon. Similarly, you may state that Sir Richard Branson flaunted his wealth and flamboyance by buying a private island and as a result, the press started to give more coverage to the business tycoon.

However, you need not rely only on your business achievements to link your individual story with your brand. If you seek to create a founder's legend, you need to identify and highlight unique aspects of your personality. Your unique traits will be eventually associated with the brand as well.

You can chronicle your achievements, qualifications and vision when you describe about yourself. Similarly, you can highlight any detours that you may have taken before you started your company or brand. Finally, you can also describe your shortcomings or the instances when you did not achieve the expected objectives. Your individual journey will assign a character or a personality to your brand as well.

Customers will begin to perceive your brand with qualities that you possess. We can build and sustain founder's legend for our brands using digital platforms such as official website, social media handles, podcasts and YouTube channels.

Product Storytelling

Coca Cola is one of the most popular soft drink companies in the world. We can discover the iconic white Coca Cola typography over red background even in the most remote corners of the planet. However, apart from the legendary soft drink, the company is also famous for its highly publicized yet top-secret formula to create the beverage.

The formula for creating the Coca Cola soft drink has been a closely guarded secret ever since the company came into existence in the year 1891. Information available on the public domain suggests that there is only one written copy of the formula. This written copy is now stored in a highly secured and a massive vault at the World of Coca Cola museum in Atlanta. The secret formula, an ingredient in Coca Cola is now a legend in itself.

Coca Cola is not the only company that uses a secret ingredient to create its popular products. Colonel Harland Sanders used the top-secret original recipe to prepare the famous fried chicken. This recipe comprises of a blend of 11 herbs and spices. The original recipe is signed by Colonel Sanders himself and is now stored in a secured vault at the KFC headquarters in Louisville. Like the secret formula of Coca Cola, KFC's original recipe is one of the most closely guarded trade secrets in America.

A good story always has an element of mystery or secrecy. This secret component motivates any reader to continue to engage with the story. Any company would require a set of raw materials or ingredients in order to manufacture a product. Often, companies promote the finished product in order to create a brand in the market. However, we can also shift our focus to the often-unnoticed raw materials or ingredients in order to project our product as a formidable brand. The highly publicized yet closely guarded trade secrets transformed Coca Cola and KFC into legendary brands.

Preconscious mind values scarcity or rarity. This behaviour enabled the primitive man to understand and to cherish the value of things that were difficult to obtain in the external environment. Similarly, the preconscious mind notices and is in awe of things that are mysterious or secret. One of the powerful ways by which companies can transform their brands into legends is by letting the market know that they use a top-secret or a mysterious component to manufacture the product. The consumers will soon start to follow the trail of information related to the secret or mysterious component of the brand.

You need not wrap your process that you utilize to create your product in a cloak of secrecy in order to differentiate your brand. The process of creating a product or even sourcing the raw materials can uniquely position the brand. The way by which you manufacture your product or the extent to which you go to acquire the specific raw materials for your product can portray your brand as a uniquely crafted work of art instead of being perceived by customers as another generic product.

Starbucks exemplifies how even a generic beverage like coffee can be positioned as an exotic brand. Starbucks declares boundless curiosity and passion for everything related to coffee. Starbucks experiments with processes such as roasting, brewing, aging, infusing and distilling to create a range of masterpieces.

The company also provides guidance for various processes that can be used for brewing coffee beans such as pour-over, coffee press and siphon.

Starbucks sources coffee beans from various corners of the world to create new varieties of coffee. The company sources high quality Arabica beans from the Lam Dong province in Central Vietnam to create the Vietnam Da Lat coffee. Similarly, the company creates Colombia Pedregal coffee from the beans that are grown by farmers in the volcanic soil of Pedregal province in Colombia.

Brands can demonstrate authenticity and uniqueness through the process that they use to create the product and through the method by which they source the raw materials or ingredients. As a result, brand definition is no longer restricted to the final product. Instead, companies can utilize the raw materials or the production processes to position the brand in a unique manner. We can project our brand as a work of art by highlighting the focus on the extent to which we can go to source specific raw materials. Similarly, we can point out as to how we incorporate unique production processes that ensure a high quality product.

Preconscious mind always approves of attention to detail. If a company goes out of the way to describe how it sources its raw materials or how it uses unique technologies to manufacture a product, the customer will perceive the fine details as a validation of high quality. When we include uniqueness during any stage of the production process, we can highlight this quality to differentiate our brand as well. The preconscious mind always looks out for novel objects in the environment.

Customer Storytelling

A single dad raising three kids from Los Angeles decided to list an extra room in his home on Airbnb. This allowed him to spend more time with his family and provided him with a source of income. Finally, this customer was able to connect with new guests using Airbnb.

Another person from Japan has travelled to 38 countries over 200 days. This customer uses Airbnb to select a place to stay whenever he travels to another country. He says that he can meet with local people and learn more about their lives and traditions by using Airbnb to book a room whenever he goes on a vacation.

Customers are pivotal to any business or brand and hence customer stories can validate and establish a brand.

Customer stories can be as simple as a two-line text review of the form. Companies can also represent a customer story in a visual format. One of the most simple yet elegant visual forms of customer stories are the before and after images that we would have seen for various products in the infomercials aired on late night cable television.

Some customer stories go beyond stating reviews or testimonials. Stories such as those of Airbnb brand provide more details about how the product made a significant impact in the lives of customers.

Customers primarily seek information about a brand by reading reviews, testimonials or stories about other individuals who have interacted with the brand. However, the preconscious mind also seeks social approval and validation for a brand by looking out for customer stories.

The preconscious mind also removes the novelty factor associated with a brand by processing the relevant customer stories. Customer stories are important not only for new customers who are thinking about trying a brand but also for existing customers who may want to update themselves about the current brand stature in the market.

Customer loyalty towards a brand might shift when the customer discovers new and conflicting stories about the product or service. Even a single customer story can have a disproportionate impact on the brand. Customer stories that highlight shabby customer service or mediocre product performance often trend and go viral on social media. This phenomenon creates an immediate and negative impact on the brand.

Positive customer stories that are focused on acts of generosity, kindness or empathy can boost the credibility of the brand among current as well as new customers. When a pilot for Southwest Airlines refused to fly for nearly 12 minutes in order to wait for a distressed person who wanted to travel in order to meet his ailing grandson, the incident attracted widespread and positive press coverage. The company supported the pilot's actions thereby sending the message that the management trusted the decisions and actions of its employees. The airlines would have most likely more than made up for the losses incurred from delaying one flight by winning more customers and by further bolstering brand loyalty in the industry with the coverage of this story.

Customer stories are carved in the digital space for years. These stories will set the expectations for the brand.

Companies can easily track customer stories on digital platforms to get a better understanding of how the brand is perceived in the market. Companies can track Google reviews or feedbacks on social media applications such as Twitter or Facebook to analyse the key areas in which the brand is faring well as well as the domains where the brand needs to improve.

Any opinion about a brand is entrenched in the preconscious mind of a customer through various stories. Founder's legend, product stories and customer stories play an important role in shaping the narrative about the brand among the customers. Although a customer can relate a brand to many stories, it is also crucial for companies to define the brand identity or the brand narrative. A brand identity signifies the deeper meaning for the customers. Companies can indicate to the customer the core purpose of a brand with the brand identity or narrative. We will use the BrandChakra™ framework for this purpose.

THE BRANDCHAKRA™ FRAMEWORK

Why do we as consumers use any product or service? The obvious answer would be that we have a functional need and we meet that requirement by paying for a product or service. However, what makes us prefer one brand of product or service to others? What makes us loyal customers of one brand? You may think that our preconscious minds has learned motor skills or muscle memories associated with a brand and hence when we wish to purchase a product or service fulfil our requirements, we rely on our preconscious minds to select a preferred brand.

We live in a world that is inundated with information everywhere. We view advertisements on television and YouTube channels. Newspapers are full of advertisements. Smartphone Apps contain small sections to display information about various brands as well. Companies talk about their products or services through strategic product placement even in movies as well. The preconscious mind of an average consumer is overwhelmed with information about various brands.

How does the preconscious mind of any average consumer process this deluge of digital and print information? How does a consumer picks a brand from a large variety of options that are available to him/her? The answer lies in the fundamental priorities of the preconscious mind – preferring speed over efficiency and tracking emotional responses to select a response.

We do not want to engage our precious cognitive faculties to analyse every single bit of information about various brands that are available before we finally purchase a product or service. Instead, our preconscious mind prefers to use a key shortcut to select a brand. This shortcut is to analyse the emotional response expected from a brand.

Expected emotional outcomes from a product or service enables our preconscious mind to determine an ideal response. As a result, we will either prefer, reject or ignore the brand. The emotional outcome after experiencing a product or service will play critical role for a consumer when he evaluates a brand. Similarly, the preconscious mind looks out for the deeper meaning or significance for any brand whenever the consumer is evaluating various choices.

BrandChakra™ - A framework to design brand identities

Consumers do not view their interaction with a product or service from a purely transactional service. Instead, consumers search for deeper meaning from their experiences with brands. An identity defines what a brand stands for. This brand identity provides an inherent purpose to the products or services. A brand identity also outlines the emotional outcomes that customers can expect from using a product or service.

Hence, a Harley Davidson bike is not just a two-wheeler vehicle that is used for transportation, for its loyal customers. The bike means energy and dynamism for the customers. Likewise, Apple stands for creativity and innovation. As a result, customers are willing to pay a huge premium and are eager to purchase the next version of Apple smartphones, laptops or tablets.

Good politicians intuitively understand the importance of identity. Politicians often emphasize on what they stand for. As a result, politicians always try to shape their election campaigns around one core theme or narrative. Barack Obama successfully fought the US presidential elections on the core idea of bringing change to the country. Similarly, real estate tycoon turned politician Donald Trump fought the last presidential elections on the themes of America First and making America great again. Unflinching patriotism defined the political brand of Donald Trump that eventually helped him to score a surprise win in the intensely fought contest.

We have observed earlier as to how emotions can alter the physiology or the inner systems of a human being. We have also seen that emotions can communicate with the preconscious mind and as a result, play a key role in establishing learned motor responses for any human being. An identity can enable a brand to elicit the appropriate emotional responses for a consumer. A brand that can create the expected emotional outcomes will be able to establish learned motor responses in the preconscious mind of a customer. The learned responses will in turn make the brand a default or preferred choice for the customer.

Customers do not become brand loyalists just based on the functions, features or benefits that are offered by the brand. Customers will vouch for those brands that offer a deeper meaning and purpose.

BrandChakra™ is a framework or a model that we can use to design the identity for any brand. This model comprises of levels that can define what the brand represents or stands for. These levels will enable the brand to provide an inner meaning that can resonate with the customers at a deeper level. You can use the BrandChakra™ model to define your brand or to analyse competitor brands. You can use BrandChakra™ to differentiate and to position your brand in a unique manner in the market. Finally, you can use the model to design new marketing campaigns that can relaunch a brand with a new identity.

You can choose any one or a combination of levels from the BrandChakra™ framework to define your brand identity. The level or combination of levels that you extract from the model can be used to design the core idea, theme or concept for your brand. You can use one level to define a singular core identity for your brand or you can build your brand identity around a package of ideas created with various levels to create one central theme.

The levels that you use from the BrandChakra™ framework to define your brand can have significant implications on your product or service design, packaging specifications, print communications as well as digital marketing strategies. Your brand identity will be pivotal in determining whether your product or service attracts enough customers in order to dominate the market.

You can use the framework not only to design unique identities for your product or service brand but also to define the core idea for other applications across various functions in your organization.

For e.g. suppose you are heading the Human Resources function in your organization. Your company's business strategy requires top-notch talent for execution. Your objective is to attract high quality candidates from across the country to fill the various positions in your company. You can use the various levels from the BrandChakra™ model to design a unique employee value proposition that can position your company as a preferred employer among the candidates.

Similarly, you can use the model to define the core idea for an organization wide skill building training program.

This core idea can then establish the training program as a flagship exercise to look forward. As a result, you can attract greater participation from the employees thereby ensuring that the training program is an organization wide success.

You can also apply the various levels in the model to design a unique narrative for various corporate social responsibility or CSR campaigns that your organization might launch. Instead of projecting various CSR events as separate activities, you can use the framework to create one core idea or concept for your CSR campaign. You can then introduce individual CSR events that belong to the same category as a part of one campaign.

Finally, you can use the BrandChakra™ model to revamp or to relaunch your existing brand with a new concept or narrative. You may also conduct several marketing campaigns across various platforms such as print or digital as a part of your overall brand building exercise. You can use this framework to design various themes or ideas for individual marketing campaigns before you test the campaign performance among the target audience.

The following image defines the BrandChakra™ model:

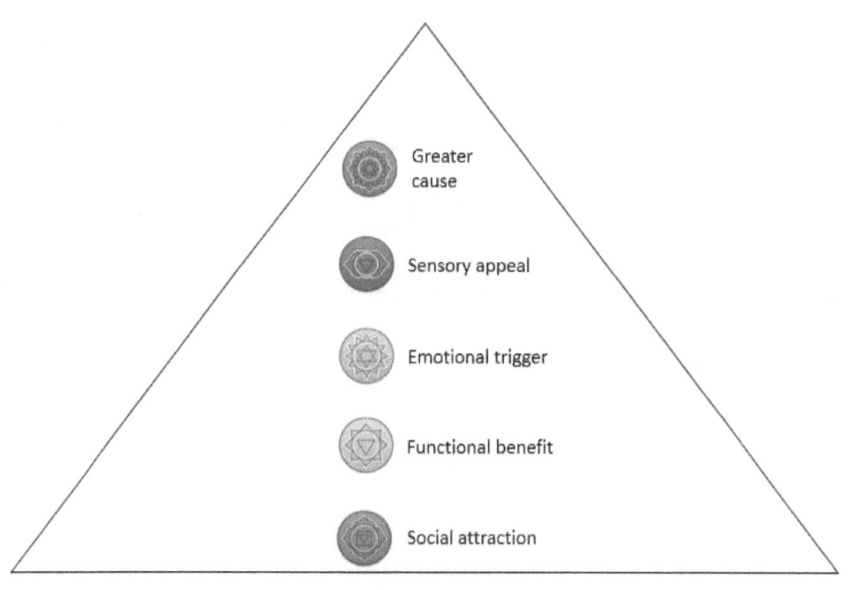

The BrandChakra™ model

Social attraction, Functional benefit, Emotional trigger, Sensory appeal and Greater cause are the different levels in the BrandChakra™ model as shown in the above image. Each level has its own significance in terms of application and is independent of other levels in the models. We will look into the details of each level in the model in the subsequent sections.

SOCIAL ATTRACTION

What are the most important objectives for a human being that has been relevant since the prehistoric times? You may mention that hunting for food, gathering resources and seeking security have been the most crucial and enduring objectives for the humankind. However, one more critical objective has defined and shaped the actions and behaviours of humans. The need to attract an ideal partner to start a family. Average males have a need to look and feel attractive in order to appear appealing enough in the society to attract the ideal partner.

Similarly, females prioritize attractiveness in order to project themselves as the ideal choice for the male counterpart. The need to attract a partner and to start a family is primal in nature among human beings.

A possible evolutionary reason for this tendency could be the need for prehistoric human beings to seek safety in numbers. The cave dwelling man as a solitary being could not have survived the harsh external environment that were full of hostile predators. As a result, the ancient human being joined forces with other humans to form a rudimentary group or tribe. Similarly, the prehistoric alpha male sought a partner to start a family and to extend his lineage.

What are the two most important criteria for males in order to make themselves appealing enough to attract a life partner? One is physical attractiveness and the other one is material success. A male who is physically attractive sends a subtle signal to prospective female partners that he is healthy enough to start a family. Likewise, material success for any male indicates his ability to provide for and to sustain a family to potential candidates from which one can become his partner.

Similarly, females consider the need to feel attractive as one of the most crucial goals in order to obtain an ideal partner. Males consider attractiveness as a subtle indicator that the female is healthy enough to become his partner and to start a family. The need to attract is visceral in nature and this need has sustained from the Stone Age up to the present.

Companies have utilized this need to attract among consumers by shaping their brand narratives around this proposition. When a South African bank tried to promote its loan business, it tried various combinations of loan interest rates as well as other materials related to the brochure before sending the loan offer documents to 50000 customers through direct mail package.

One of the key findings of this study was that when the bank included the image of a female in the loan offer documents that were sent to male customers, the response rate increased by the same amount as a 4.5 percent drop in the loan interest rate. However, the image of the female on the loan offer document did not have any significant impact on female customers. Thus, a simple photo of female caused a change in response equivalent to a nearly five percent drop in the loan interest rate.

In yet another study, researchers showed male participants images of scantily clad girls.

Later, researchers asked these participants either to choose an amount immediately or to negotiate a bigger sum of money after a week or month. In each test, participants who viewed the images chose delayed reward amounts lower than the amount selected by other participants who did not view the images. This study demonstrates that the male subjects, who are primed by suggestive images of females, are willing to make impulsive decisions for immediate gratification.

Brands can make themselves an object of attraction or they can project themselves as the solution for consumers to project themselves as attractive, successful or worthy enough to attract fascinating life partners. Social attraction level of our model can be used in this regard in order to shape the brand identity as required.

We can utilize the social attraction level of the BrandChakra™ model to design the brand narrative in such a way that consumers may perceive the product or service from the following two perspectives:

1. The brand itself is an object of attraction and thus a customer has to purchase this brand.

2. The brand can make us look or feel attractive. Thus, a customer has to purchase this brand because the customer thinks that this brand will make him attractive in the society. The customer thinks this in turn will help him to attract good life partners.

The first perspective for perceiving a product or service is important whenever the brand is not directly linked to providing attractiveness or beauty to the consumers. For e.g. a banking service such as personal loans has little relevance to making any consumer attractive. However, if you add a photo of attractive female as a banking executive explaining the terms of loan in the brochure or promotional video, the preconscious mind of a potential customer will perceive the loan service itself to be attractive. Now you may wonder what to do if there are female customers to whom you want to offer loan. In such cases, perhaps you can experiment with including a photo of attractive male as a banking executive. Hence, you can tweak the promotional content for your brand with different variables to check what works best.

The intention to transform a brand itself into an object of attraction plays a key role in the concept of celebrity endorsements. An attractive supermodel or a film star lends her own charm and personality to the brand. As a result, customers perceive the brand itself to be attractive and an object of desire.

The second perspective that we saw earlier was to shape the brand identity in such a way that the product or service is perceived by the consumers to be an instrument in making them look or feel attractive. In this case, we are not aiming for making the brand itself an object of desire or attraction. Instead, we intend to tell the customer that if you use this brand, you will look or feel attractive.

Attraction in this case is not just restricted to physical beauty or charm. Material success, wealth or social status can also make an individual equally attractive in the modern society. You can apply the social attraction level of the BrandChakra™ model in this case to send a message to your prospective customers that your brand will empower them to look or feel attractive. Attraction could be based on physical charm or material success.

Unilever, the global consumer goods giant, has perfected the concept of projecting brands as instruments that will make the consumer attractive. Closeup is a gel toothpaste brand of Unilever. Following is the image of a Closeup toothpaste pack that is displayed on the official website for the brand.

The product description for the toothpaste mentions that a consumer can obtain fresher breath by using Closeup. The description goes on to state that you can get the confidence with fresher breath to get up close for intense moments of closeness. The toothpaste offers fresh breath as a way to feel attractive.

Even the package for Closeup toothpaste contains elements that indicate the brand is essential to make a consumer feel attractive. Image of the smiling couple, red colour that indicate passion or desire, and the word Red Hot all signify that this toothpaste is all that you need in order to become attractive enough to attract potential partners.

Closeup has used the concept of fresh breath as a means to become attractive and to get close with potential partners. The brand shifted its identity from a provider of oral hygiene to an instrument that increases the attractiveness of its users with fresh breath. Once the brand identity was established, the various attributes of the product such as the tooth paste colour and package elements followed suit. As a result, the brand provided a coherent and deep meaning to the consumers.

Closeup is not the only brand that has created its identity on the premise of enabling consumers to become attractive. Axe body spray is another brand of Unilever that has unabashedly positioned itself as the product that men must use to become attractive. The official website for the Axe brand describes that men must add Axe body spray to their grooming arsenal in order to smell great especially during occasions such as date nights or late nights.

The brand identity for Axe body spray is based on strengthening the attractiveness of men by ensuring that they smell great. The typical advertisement for Axe body spray follows this premise – an ordinary person is unnoticed. He uses Axe body spray and as a result, women are attracted to him.

To summarize, you can apply the social attraction level of the BrandChakra™ by analysing your brand using the following steps:

1. Is your product or service directly related to benefits such as grooming, cosmetic, wellness,

hygiene or fitness? If so, you can define the brand identity as an instrument to make the target consumer look or feel attractive.

2. Is your product a consumable such as a food item or a beverage? If so, you can redefine the brand identity by stating that this product tastes or contains an ingredient that makes consumers feel attractive, thereby enabling them to get closer to their partners. For e.g. Cadbury Dark Chocolate product description states that it is the perfect item to share and to make any moment more delicious.

3. If your product or service is completely unrelated to any benefit that a consumer may derive by looking or feeling attractive, then you can turn the product or service itself into an object of desire or

attraction. Place the image of an attractive female or male model on your product brochures or pamphlets. The beauty or the charm of your models in the product or service brochures will soon radiate onto the brand itself thereby making it the object of attraction.

Every human being has an innate need to look or to feel attractive in order to get close to his/her object of desire. You can shape a powerful identity for your brand around this enduring need among consumers. The next level of the model creates the brand identity around what matters the most for consumers- benefits from the brand.

FUNCTIONAL BENEFIT

The preconscious mind is self-centred by nature. The preconscious mind will process any sensory input and choose a response in such a way that the individual is benefited from the choice. The preconscious mind will simply ignore any sensory input that is unrelated to any benefit for the individual. Thus, the preconscious mind is relentless and selfish before deciding the right response for any individual. The preconscious mind will attempt to assess the benefits for any sensory input before selecting an ideal response.

Core Benefits

Functional benefit level of the BrandChakra™ model taps on to the default behaviour of the preconscious mind to assess the benefits for any consumer before selecting an ideal response for any sensory input. The functional benefit level of the model emphasizes on how the brand will benefit the customer through various features that are available in the product or service.

When we clearly state the benefits for our brand, we enable the preconscious mind of any consumer to process the benefits of using our product or service. We have observed earlier that our preconscious mind prefers speed to efficiency and has a bias for simplicity while processing any sensory input. Functional benefit level of our model enables these tendencies among consumers.

The perceived benefits from any product or service for a consumer can be classified into the following categories:

1. Removes pain

2. Provides pleasure

3. Saves time

4. Saves money

When we analyse our brand, we can map the features of our product or service to the benefits that belong to any of the four categories that are listed above. We may often see companies focusing only on the features of their products or services. However, unless companies translate these features into tangible benefits, the preconscious minds of consumers would not consider it necessary to process the features of the brand to choose a response. We can make things easier for consumers by focusing on their benefits first and not on the product or service related features.

The electronic appliances brands focuses on primarily highlighting the product benefits. Customers do not purchase electronic appliances such as refrigerators or washing machines often. However, when the customers do purchase one, they spend a significant amount of money. Hence, these customers naturally look out for benefits before purchasing any brand.

Another area where we can observe the emphasis on functional benefits is the B2B or commercial marketing of products, services or solutions. Individuals responsible for purchasing commercial solutions for their organizations utilize the budget allocated to them for this purpose. Many of these solutions are expensive and these purchases influence the company bottom line. As a result, companies selling commercial solutions specifically focus on benefits that the customers can obtain.

Appliance with features

Following are some of the points that the company mentions for the 6 kg Samsung front loading washing machine in the official website.

1. Save huge amount of energy by washing large loads at low temperatures.

2. Remove difficult stains on clothes with unique technology.

3. Delivers superior energy efficiency and enduring performance with digital inverter motor.

4. Save time and avoid cost of calling engineer by using the automatic error monitoring system from a smartphone app.

5. Save time with quick wash program.

We can observe from the above list of points that every product feature is preceded by a specific benefit for the customer. We can also note that every benefit belongs to one of the core perceived benefits that a customer seeks from any product or service such as removing pain, saving time and saving money. As a result, the benefits resulting from each product function or feature seems relevant to the customer.

We have often seen companies who provide a laundry list of features related to their products. For e.g. when you look at some of the smartphones that are available for sale on Amazon, you would note that some of these brands emphasize on specifications such as camera pixels, operating system and memory storage. Instead, it is prudent to map tangible customer benefit to a product feature.

This phenomenon to focus almost exclusively on the various features of a company's product or solution is also widely seen during sales pitches or presentations. Marketing or sales teams often start their presentations with an overview of their product or solution. This is usually followed by the detailed list of product features. Finally, the presentation covers the customer perspective.

However, we have observed earlier that our preconscious mind is extremely self-centred and is focused on speed when it comes to processing sensory inputs. Similarly, our preconscious mind seeks to conserve the precious cognitive resources by ignoring any sensory input that is not related to a direct benefit for the individual. Hence, it is beneficial for companies to immediately highlight the core benefits that a brand can offer to a customer.

Power of free benefits

The word free has a special meaning for every consumer. Prehistoric human beings were primarily hunter-gatherers foraging for food and other resources. Hence, the cave dwellers were always on the lookout for any resource that is easy to obtain. This is because the preconscious mind quickly notes and responds to any stimuli that is novel and that appears safe. As a result, we are naturally attuned to keep track of objects that we can acquire effortlessly.

When a company offers something free, the consumer will notice the offer because his preconscious mind is primed to search for easy rewards. Hence, companies can provide some relevant accessory or service for free in order to draw the attention of the consumer towards the brand. The consumer will perceive the free offer in itself as an additional benefit that is offered by the brand. A free offer appears novel and appealing enough to attract consumers towards the brand.

Studies have demonstrated the impact of free offers on consumer behaviour. In one such study, more than two thirds of participants chose an inexpensive chocolate that the researchers offered for free over a premium chocolate that was available at a reduced price. However, when the researchers asked participants to pay a nominal price for the inexpensive chocolate instead of offering it for free, nearly 75 percent of the participants selected the premium chocolate. Hence, free offer takes precedence over the inherent value of a product in the preconscious mind of consumers.

Another popular example of the power of free offer is that of Amazon. When the ecommerce giant offered free shipping on the purchase of second book, every country barring France showed a spike in sales resulting from the offer. When the company investigated the issue, it discovered that the customers in France had to pay a nominal shipping charge on the purchase of the second book instead of free shipping, as was the case in other countries. As a result, there was no significant increase in sales resulting from the offer. When the company finally changed the offer in France to free shipping, sales also increased significantly.

The power of free offer overrides any tendency of consumer to analyse and to derive the inherent value of any product or service. Free offer can quickly draw the attention of consumers towards any brand.

Bundled Pricing

Researchers at the Carnegie Mellon and Stanford Universities have discovered that when consumers pay for something, the regions of the consumers' brain related to pain are activated. Hence, consumers literally feel pain when they pay for a product or service.

Researchers also discovered that the extent of pain that consumers experience on paying for something also depends upon the context as well as the fairness of the entire transaction. Hence, a consumer might be willing to pay hundreds of dollars for a music system that comes along with a luxury car that may cost thousands of dollars. However, the same consumer might haggle over the price of audio system when he buys it separately.

Thus, consumer experiences varied levels of pain when paying for an object depending upon the context. A hundred dollar audio system might mean a significant amount to the consumer who is buying the product separately. However, the cost of the same audio system may not mean a lot to the consumer who is buying the product along with an automobile.

Similarly, a consumer might be willing to pay a huge sum of money for an Armani jacket but the same consumer will seek the appropriate price for a jacket made by a relatively unknown company. Here, the consumer considers the high price for Armani jacket as fair because of the premium value of the brand itself. However, in other cases, the consumer seeks inherent value in the product through its features or characteristics in order to justify the price and to consider the deal as fair.

Hence, companies offer various payment and credit options to customers for purchasing a product or service. Payment by credit card delays the pain that consumers would have experienced if they had to pay for a product or service immediately. Similarly, customers can experience less pain if companies combine and offer different products or services as a part of single package instead of asking the customers to pay for every individual item. Companies can use bundled pricing or offering products or services as one package with multiple components instead of offering individual products separately.

However, you can justify a higher price for your product or service as fair if you can shape your brand identity in such a way that a premium price seems justified and fair.

Applying functional benefit level

To summarize, we can apply the functional benefit level of the BrandChakra™ model to design our brand identity by performing the following steps:

1. Identify the various features or functions offered by your product or service.

2. Identify what your target customers seek from purchasing the product or service. Classify the needs of your target customers into any of the four categories such as removing pain, providing pleasure, saving time or saving money.

3. Map each of the feature offered by your product or service against the specific needs of your target customers. Each of the feature that you highlight must offer a precise benefit to your customers.

4. Shape the value proposition of your product or service in the following manner "Experience a

specific benefit (that removes pain, provides pleasure, saves time or saves money) from a feature that is available in our product or service". Highlight a tangible benefit for the customer before mentioning the underlying feature in your product or service that delivers this benefit.

5. Include free offers such as accessories or after sales service when you are promoting your brand. Reduce purchase related pains for your customers by offering different payment and credit options.

A brand can become a preferred choice by offering specific benefits to address customer needs. However, a brand that can directly prime a customer to experience an emotional outcome can dominate the market as well.

EMOTIONAL TRIGGER

We have observed earlier that emotional outcomes can directly alter the physiology of any human being. We have seen that the internal responses triggered by the autonomous nervous system and by experiencing various emotions are similar. Emotions play a key role in communicating with the preconscious mind. The preconscious mind determines the learned motor responses or muscle memories depending upon the emotional outcomes that it either seeks or prefers to avoid.

Emotions like happiness, joy, achievement or success are universal in nature. This provides a common language for the brands to communicate with their customers. The preconscious mind experiences the emotions when a consumer interprets the emotions that are expressed along with the brand.

When we project together the brand related stimuli and the target emotion that we seek to induce in a customer, the preconscious mind will soon associate the two. Subsequently, the consumers will start to correlate the brand with the target emotion. This phenomenon occurs because the preconscious minds of consumers are primed to anticipate the target emotion when they receive the brand related stimuli. A brand strongly associated with a target emotion can create legions of loyal customers.

One of the key benefits of associating a specific emotion with a brand is that your brand is not vulnerable even when your competitors emulate the features that are available in your product or service. For e.g. many companies can provide smartphone with same features and design as that of an Apple iPhone. However, the Apple brand is widely associated with the emotion of innovation and creativity. It is difficult for competitors to associate their smartphone brand with similar emotions that are related to innovation and creativity. Hence, the Apple brand has a strategic advantage thanks to the emotional outcomes that consumers anticipate from the brand.

Starbucks is another brand that benefits from the emotions that consumers associate with the product. The ambience of a typical Starbucks cafe, the variety of coffee that are available and the process of brewing as well as serving coffee signify the emotions of trendiness and style among consumers. Other competitors may provide similar coffee but it will be difficult for them to replicate the exact emotional outcomes that consumers experience from Starbucks.

We can apply the emotional trigger level from the BrandChakra™ model to associate a brand with targeted emotional outcomes. A consumer may interact with a brand across various touchpoints. For e.g. if a consumer purchases an iPhone, he interacts with the brand at many levels such as opening the box, starting the phone for the first time, trying the various features that are available in the phone, testing the earphones for listening to music, taking a picture and so on. We can use the emotional trigger level from the framework to identify whether we can convey a specific emotion across different stages of a consumer journey.

Similarly, when a consumer interacts with a service brand, the nature of touch points may differ. For e.g. if a consumer interacts with a Starbucks brand, he/she will first visit the cafe. The consumer can experience a range of emotions during the course of his interaction with various aspects of the brand.

The consumer will then experience the different elements of the cafe such as lighting, colours of various objects such as walls or furniture, any music playing in the background and so on. Subsequently, the consumer will look into the menu and will order a coffee. Finally, the consumer will drink the coffee and will pay for the bill.

In this case, the environment in the cafe, the coffee itself and customer service are some of the key touchpoints where the consumer interacts with the brand and experiences certain emotional outcomes. We can apply the emotional trigger level from our model in order to determine how to project a target emotion across various touchpoints of interaction between the consumer and a service brand. A company can aim to provide a consistent emotional outcome for a customer during the course of his interaction with the brand.

We need to apply the required emotional trigger with a brand in a comprehensive manner across various touchpoints in order to entrench the association between the brand and the target emotion. This will prime the preconscious minds of consumers to expect the targeted emotional outcome from a brand related stimuli.

Bonded by brotherhood

Human being is a social animal. Any individual craves for social belonging and togetherness. This need for bonding is the cornerstone for collective groups such as tribes, faiths and nations. Individuals unite and form groups based on sharing few key attributes. For e.g. citizens of one nation can share some common characteristics such as belonging to same geography, speaking the same language or agreeing to one political system. Fraternity or brotherhood is a powerful emotional trigger that transcends age or social status. Companies can seek to associate the resilient emotion of brotherhood with their brands. The objective can be to motivate individual consumers for establishing a community or a wide-ranging group in order to interact with a brand.

Soccer clubs, especially the ones from Europe, realize the importance of forming a community or a brotherhood around their brands. Any soccer club comprise of various aspects such as:

1. Club logo and history of jerseys

2. Home stadium or venue

3. City of origin

4. Club history in terms of number of tournaments played or won

5. Players who have played for the club so far as well as the current team

Each of these aspects play a major role in forming a tribe or community around a soccer club. As a result, a person living in Shanghai or Manila can become an ardent follower of Manchester United. The brand of the club can now invite loyalists from distant lands.

Some companies have successfully cultivated a community of dedicated followers for their brands. This community not only creates a legendary status for the brand but also inspires other prospective customers to join the tribe.

Royal Enfield is the oldest motorcycle brand in the world that is still in production. Royal Enfield motorcycles are sold in more than 50 countries. The company factories located in Chennai, India manufactures different series of the Royal Enfield motorbike such as Bullet 350,

Himalayan and Thunderbird. Loyal customers of the brand from various cities and towns in India have come together to form local groups and communities. These groups frequently go on road trips. Finally, these groups inspire others to purchase a Royal Enfield bike and to become a part of the growing community.

LEGO Group is another company that has inspired numerous communities around the world. The company works with its fans in the area of co-creation, content and campaigns. Brand loyalists share their ideas by utilizing more than 260 independent fan sites and an official crowd-sourcing platform called as Cuusoo. Finally, anyone can become a LEGO fan designer by submitting an idea to the company. The company experts review an idea once it has gathered 10000 supporters. LEGO Fan designers can then collaborate with the company designers to finalize a set that will be finally ready for stores.

Communities inspire the emotion of camaraderie. Communities can engage with the brand in various ways in order to reinforce their dedication to the product. This dedicated tribe acts as brand advocates in the society.

To summarize, we can apply the emotional trigger level of the BrandChakra™ model to associate our brand with target emotions. We can perform the following steps in this regard.

1. Identify the different touchpoints or instances when the customers interact with your product or service. Compile the complete customer experience with your brand into a journey map.

2. Determine an empowering emotional trigger or outcome that you want your brand to be

associated with. Some of these emotional outcomes could be joy, achievement or friendliness.

3. Map the emotional outcome to the different touchpoints when the customer interacts with the brand. Revamp the elements of interaction at these touchpoints to ensure that the customer experiences a consistent emotional outcome from the brand. These elements could be product or package design in case of product related brands. The elements of interaction in case of touchpoints related to a service could be ambience or customer support. Test the customer experience with various touchpoints to determine the emotional outcomes at various points of interaction with the brand.

4. Foster a sense of community among your brand's customers by asking for feedback. Seek ideas for new products from your customers or ask customers to post pictures or to share stories of how they interact with the brand.

Brands can dominate the preconscious minds of consumers by inducing targeted emotional outcomes. However, companies can also utilize a variety of sensory stimuli to design a complete brand experience.

SENSORY APPEAL

Human beings are equipped with five senses namely sight, sound, smell, taste and touch. Our preconscious mind processes inputs or stimuli that it obtains from various sensory organs. Subsequently, the preconscious mind determines the ideal motor response for these sensory inputs.

Many brands in the market today are dependent on sight based sensory input to attract the attention of consumers. Many of these brands would rely on a unique logo, typeface or a brand name in order to project themselves as appealing enough to the market. However, as global branding and marketing expert Martin Lindstrom suggests, companies can create a unique signature for their brands across all sensory inputs. A brand that can be identified not only by its visual identity but also by the way it smells, tastes, or is heard will have a significant competitive advantage.

How do we identify a brand when we look at it? We will initially look at the logo design and the brand name. Subsequently, we will try to interpret other elements that are related to the brand such as background colours, font type and font size. Our preconscious mind will process these visual inputs in a fraction of a second. Soon, the consumer will associate the packaging style, product design and other elements such as font type or different colours with the brand.

However, we have also seen earlier that our preconscious mind has a simplicity bias when it processes sensory inputs. As a result, our preconscious mind has to expend many cognitive resources when it is overwhelmed with numerous sensory stimuli.

Companies often go overboard by cluttering the visual space for their brands. Sometimes, the package would be cluttered with a lot of information related to the product. In other instances, the product package would comprise of a lot of colours or graphical elements. You can provide the essence of your brand identity with simplicity and elegance. You can ensure that the consumers do not have to process a lot of information in order to understand the core features or meaning of your brand.

For e.g. what do you see when you go to Google home page? The web page is mostly empty. The centre of the page comprises of a Google logo, a text box for entering the search query and two buttons for starting the internet search. The preconscious mind of any user does not have to process many elements when he visits the Google home page. Hence, the Google home page favours the simplicity bias of the preconscious mind.

In contrast, do you remember the home page for Yahoo? The website would have the logo, text box and search buttons towards the top centre side of the page. The rest of the page comprised of numerous links to other sites such as Sports, Finance and so on. The consumer would have a lot of information to process by looking at the website. The Yahoo home page did not favour the simplicity expectation of an average preconscious mind.

To summarize, we can make a brand more noteworthy when we focus on simplicity for visual elements. Simplicity would enable the preconscious mind of a consumer to associate a brand with various visual elements such as logo, colours and fonts.

Music to ears

Experts from United Kingdom conducted a study to understand the impact of background sound on consumer buying behaviour. The researchers chose a wine shop to perform this experiment. The researchers played French and German background music on alternating days in the wine shop. The results of the study revealed an interesting pattern. French and German origin wines showed significant sales on the day the wine shop played a matching background music. Another study measured how a customer's perception about the bank changed with the inclusion of a background music. The results showed that when the background included a classical sound track, customers perceived the bank to be inspiring. Hence, the results of these studies show that preconscious minds of consumers can correlate various sounds to the overall brand experience.

Many companies have incorporated an audio component in their overall brand strategy. United Airlines incorporated George Gershwin's "Rhapsody in Blue" in its television campaigns. Intel included a simple five-tone musical at the end of its television advertisements. Global financial services company AXA has a collection of branded music. Each track is especially composed for the company. These tracks also contain a signature sound or audio logo. Marketing teams of the company use different kinds of music from this collection in various campaigns across 56 countries.

Paris Airport required a signature audio that combined the dreams and pleasure of the city as well as the Parisian flair along with the spirit and challenges of an international airport. Paris Airport collaborated with a French creative agency to create a unique audio sound that communicated the luxurious, magical and charismatic personality of Paris city. A passenger listens to a specific music at various touchpoints such as during the start of announcements, at terminals, boarding gates, corridors, restrooms, parking lots, over the phone and during various events. As a result, passenger experience lower perceived wait times, more enjoyable corridors and greater sense of security.

French automobile giant Renault introduced an audio identity that conveys the values of humanity and emotion when the company recently repositioned its brand with a new tagline called "Passion for Life". Huggies, which is a leading brand in baby care, included a signature audio identity that conveys the special connection between a mother and child. The company uses various versions of this audio identity in different markets around the world.

We need to explore the brands, their environments and their heritage in order to understand their visions, aspirations and strategic decisions. We can use this knowledge to create an audio identity that can describe the brand's personality to the audience. This audio identity has to be adapted for various communication touchpoints when the customer interacts with the brand.

The choices of various voices that represent the personality of the brand can also be crucial in designing a vocal identity. Voice activated searches and voice enabled assistant devices will become more commonplace in the market. Voice assisted technology will enable a brand to speak to its customers. Brands can create significant impression on the customers by using its vocal identity.

The vocal identity for a brand must consider key factors such as clarity, energy level, age, gender and accent. The vocal identity for a brand can also convey values such as friendliness, warmth, authority, leadership or expertise.

Sound is a crucial sensory stimulus that can create a significant impression on the preconscious mind. Babies respond to sounds before they are born. Audio identity should be a fundamental component of our brand strategy to connect with our customers.

Sweet smell of success

You may have often walked past bakeries, restaurants or pizza shops in your local neighbourhood or town. What do you notice when you pass by these outlets? You may have observed the name and the shop itself. Maybe you would have spotted couple of customers who are inside the shop. What would be your response to these sensory stimuli? Your preconscious mind would have noted and processed these sensory inputs and would have probably created some desire within you for pizza.

Now imagine this scenario in a slightly different context. Suppose you are walking past a bakery but this time you are also able to smell the aroma of freshly baked cakes along with observing the shop and the customers who are inside. How would your preconscious mind respond this time? You would most likely crave to eat a cake immediately.

Our autonomous nervous system can respond to any smell or aroma related stimuli in an immediate or involuntary manner. From an evolutionary perspective, when we detect an aroma, our preconscious mind infers that a related object is located nearby. Thus, the aroma can trigger an immediate desire for an object in a consumer. Hence, it is beneficial for an organization to incorporate an aroma-based identity for its brand.

An important step towards designing an aroma-based identity for any brand is to identify the smell that is most relatable to the product or service. For e.g. a store that sells shoes can be easily associated with the aroma of fresh leather. We can identify a coffee shop with the smell of freshly crushed coffee beans. A restaurant can diffuse the aroma of its most delicious dish in order to attract new customers.

In case there is no relatable aroma for a product or service, we can identify a unique fragrance that can convey the brand values. The company must also verify that the aroma is present in a subtle manner around a product or service. Consumers will find it suspicious if there is too much of a fragrance around any product or service.

Once we have determined a unique aroma for our brand, we can arrange to disperse this fragrance at suitable touchpoints when the consumer interacts with the product or service. The fragrance can come from the package or the product itself. In case of service like banking or restaurant, we can use various points within the location to spread the brand related aroma.

Fragrance enables quick response and is hence conducive for the simplicity bias of preconscious mind. Thus, it is crucial for companies to assign a unique aroma for their brands. This will enable the consumers to detect the brand from the fragrance or aroma itself.

When we combine the visual elements along with the signature audio and a unique fragrance for a brand, we can convey the presence of our brand to the preconscious mind of a consumer through various sensory stimuli. Companies can provide a holistic brand experience for their customers by incorporating elements of brand identity across different sensory inputs.

Other sensations

Touch is one of the most intimate of the five senses for any human being. We intuitively use touch to determine what is real. Consumers follow this behaviour when they shop for any product. For e.g. when customers shop for any clothes, they will touch the apparel to get a feeling for the fabric. Similarly, when a customer purchases a smartphone from a store, he will often pick up the phone to get a feel of various factors such as how the phone weighs, does the surface feels slippery, does the phone feel too wide while holding it in the hands and so on. Customers touch or hold a product to get an understanding of what the product really feels like. Companies can utilize this sensory input to design a unique identity for their brands.

For example, consider BAWLS Guarana energy drink. The company's official website displays the following image for the BAWLS Original beverage:

The glass bottle contains unique raised bumps that provides a grip. As a result, the bottle does not slip from a consumer's hands when they are wet. However, when a consumer holds a BAWLS Guarana bottle, he/she can feel the texture and infer the brand. The preconscious mind associates the product texture or design with the brand.

We can modify the product or package design to provide a unique texture or feel for the customers. However, we can also include an additional accessory with the product that can provide a unique tactile experience for the customers.

For e.g. Crown Royal is the number one Canadian whisky in the world and the sixth largest spirits brand in the United States. The brand owner Diageo provides a purple velvet pouch that comprises of gold stitching and a gold drawstring along with the Crown Royal bottle. The pouch itself has now acquired an iconic status among Crown Royal consumers. Fans have used the purple velvet pouch to create unique items such as car covers and bartender vests. These pouches are now so popular that the customers can purchase them separately.

Following is the image of the iconic Crown Royal whisky bottle along with the purple velvet pouch.

Various tactile features for your product will enable customers to experience your brand in a different way. We can include special tactile features at various levels such as the product, package or accessory to design a unique brand experience for the customers. What a customer feels when he holds the product or its package can help the preconscious mind to identify the brand.

To summarize, we can apply the sensory appeal level of the BrandChakra™ framework to create a sensation-based identity for our brands. We can perform the following steps to create a brand experience that can appeal to various sensations of a consumer.

1. Determine the personality, emotions or values that you want your brand to convey.

2. Identify the various touchpoints where the consumers interact with your brand. In case of products, some of these touchpoints could include purchasing the product from a store, opening the package, using the product and so on. In case of service, the touchpoints could include customer service, service related brochures and the establishment itself.

3. Determine the visual elements that ideally reflects your brand personality and values. These visual elements include the logo, background colours,

font type, font size and brand related description. Focus on simplicity instead of cluttering the visual space with many elements such as colours or brand related description.

4. Create a unique audio identity that represents your brand personality. Play your brand's signature audio or its variations at different touchpoints.

5. Identify an aroma that is most relatable to your product or service. This fragrance can also represent your brand's personality or values. You can then ensure that the consumers can smell the aroma related to your brand whenever they interact with your product or service. You can arrange to disperse the unique aroma related to

your brand at various touchpoints when consumers interact with your product or service.

6. Create a unique tactile based brand experience for your consumers by altering the texture of your product or package. You can also provide additional accessories for your product.

Companies can create a unique identity for their brands across different sensations. A brand with multi-sensory identity will create a coherent experience for consumers. However, brands can emerge from a pure transactional or commercial perspective and can appear to be having a greater purpose or cause for doing business.

GREATER CAUSE

Man seeks a higher purpose for his goals and actions. This purpose is greater than the mere task of accumulating wealth. Purpose defines the reason why an individual pursues a certain objective or why he accomplishes certain task.

The act of purchasing a product or preferring a brand may appear to be transactional in nature. We buy a product or service because we have a need that we seek to fulfil with a brand.

However, we can redefine brand loyalty from the perspective of a greater cause or purpose. When a company declares that it believes in a greater cause or purpose, then it includes a dimension that is bigger than business objectives or goals. Consumers will perceive a brand that believes in a noble cause or purpose to be greater than commercial aspects such as market share, revenue or profits.

There are organizations whose appeal to a target audience entirely depends upon persuading individuals to a greater cause. For e.g. armed forces in a nation that does not have a policy of conscription persuades citizens to volunteer for military service by focusing upon noble causes such as patriotism or serving for the country. Armed forces highlight salary and benefits as secondary benefits of joining the military.

Similarly, not for profit or charitable organizations persuade citizens to donate money for a cause. Charities will initially highlight the key cause for which they are working. Subsequently, these organizations will ask citizens to contribute towards addressing a cause by donating money. Charitable institutions usually provide data about how they used the money for the declared purpose. Donors have no commercial benefit from donating money to a charity. However, these donors believe in working for a greater cause and their way of doing so is to donate money to a charitable institution with a similar purpose.

We can use the greater cause level of the BrandChakra™ framework to associate our brand with a greater cause or purpose. As a result, consumers will perceive our brand to be noble as well.

Companies can assign a greater cause or purpose to their brand identities by performing the following steps:

1. Identify how your product or service brand contributes to the greater well-being of the society or environment. For e.g. Morris Garage is promoting its electric SUV in India by asking prospective customers to lead from the front, to inspire others and to start a movement for change. Highlight how your brand can specifically benefit segments of society or environment.

2. Your brand can also associate to a relatable cause by declaring your support for the same. You can collaborate with a charitable institution or you can focus your company's CSR related activities in order to work for the cause.

3. Your organization can also pledge to contribute a share of revenues resulting from a brand towards a charitable cause.

4. Promote your brand's commitment towards a charitable cause through digital marketing and official websites.

Companies can build a powerful identity for their brands by declaring their commitment towards a greater cause.

BrandChakra™ model provides a holistic framework for designing a compelling brand identity. We can create a suitable brand strategy by applying any of the levels such as social attraction, functional benefit, emotional trigger, sensory appeal or greater cause from the model. A key factor that can shape the brand narrative is the cultural expression that emerges in the external environment.

CULTURAL EXPRESSION

Dictator Ben Ali ruled over the North African country of Tunisia since 1987. Tunisia was stable and wealthy and as a result, protests were unheard of in the nation. The government discouraged dissent and suppressed political opposition.

Protests against rising poverty and political repression started across Tunisia in December 2010. These protests continued for a weeks before the country's dictator fled from the nation. The revolution was successful in Tunisia. Anti-establishment movements soon started in various nations across the Arab world.

Egyptian leader Hosni Mubarak soon faced widespread protests across the nation. His establishment was unable to suppress the protests for long and as a result, the dictator had to step down. The Arab Spring removed yet another regime. Meanwhile, violent revolutions had started in other countries with authoritarian regimes such as Libya, Syria, Yemen, Bahrain and Algeria.

The common link to all these protests were the widespread use of social media platforms such as Twitter and Facebook by the protesters. Activists used Facebook pages to organize demonstrations across various nations. Protesters uploaded videos on YouTube to broadcast the updates on the revolutions to the outside world. Similarly, hashtags and trending stories on Twitter provided the latest news about the protests. Social media became an instrument of political change.

Culture is a set of commonly expressed and shared ideas, beliefs, practices and codes. Culture or ideology, in any civilized society, is always expressed through various forms such as religion, political and government system, arts, literature and socially accepted norms. Culture allows an individual to express himself or herself at various levels. In an aspiring society, even brands are also part of the cultural expression of a customer.

Iconic and successful brands are anchored with an underlying ideology and are likely to display an emphatic cultural expression. Brands with a strong cultural expression are likely to distinguish themselves from their peers. Brands with an ideological or cultural underpinning are less likely to be competed on similar terms by rivals, who can easily replicate incremental innovations or features.

There is a dominant cultural expression in any society. However, a latent culture or subculture is also present in the fringes of any society. This subculture is waiting to express itself and to become mainstream. Observers often ignore or underestimate the pace at which a latent cultural expression will become the mainstream voice in a society. For e.g. many political experts and media outlets were largely unaware about the widespread discontent across the Arab world until the protests started.

Companies or brands in any industry portray a cultural ideology as well. Organizations usually follow the dominant cultural expression in any society when they define the identity for their brands. However, companies can discover the subcultures or latent cultural expression to design a unique identity for their brands. Social media companies like Facebook and Twitter tapped onto the latent cultural expression of public discontent in the Arab world to propel the widespread use of their platforms across the world. These companies promoted themselves as instruments of change that can start a revolution in any country. The number of users on these social media applications increased significantly. Political leaders from across the globe started posting updates on their official Facebook page and Twitter handles. Any major news story was widely debated among numerous users on these applications. These social media sites soon became popular enough to set the political narrative in any country. Facebook became more than just a platform to share pictures and to connect with friends. It became a tool to bring change. Twitter was not just about microblogging. Hashtags and trends on the application could bring widespread awareness for any issue.

To summarize, social media companies did not stick to the conventional cultural expression of technology or innovation that was prevalent in Western countries. Instead, these organizations used the latent cultural expression of the need to voice one's opinion for inspiring change. This latent cultural expression soon entered the mainstream narrative and social media companies profited from this transformation.

Nike is another brand that understood the power of latent cultural expression. The brand realized in the seventies that the American economy was facing tough competition from other countries such as Japan and West Germany. The post war economic boom was over and citizens will have to strive to be competitive. Nike shaped its brand identity around the emerging cultural expression of the need to perform and to be competitive individually.

Nike used the "Just do it" campaign to emphasize on the image of an individual performer who trains outside the limelight. The dominant cultural expression in the footwear industry was that of successful athletes who are victorious in various competitions. Nike utilized the latent cultural expression of individualism to shape its brand identity as a product that can motivate you to train and to excel.

Patanjali is another company from India that understood the power of latent cultural expression. A spiritual monk turned into an entrepreneur and started this consumer goods company. The company utilized the emerging cultural expression of patriotism and promoted itself as an Indian company that can compete with foreign companies. The company's products soon became popular among Indian consumers.

Companies can understand the latent cultural expression by performing the following steps:

1. Perform a qualitative research of the emerging political developments in the country as well as around the globe. Identify a common pattern for these political trends.

2. Understand the underlying themes that are visible in works of art, movies and literature.

3. Use the core concept that defines the latent cultural expression to design the brand identity.

You may need to explore diverse and unique sources such as YouTube comments for popular videos or subreddits when you are performing qualitative research to understand the various subcultures. A brand narrative aligned with emerging cultural expression will gain widespread acceptance among customers.

BRANDS AND CORPORATE CULTURE

Every year, companies from different industries across the world spend billions of dollars for mergers and acquisitions related deals. Companies hire expensive investment bankers and strategy consulting firms to scout for suitable targets that they either can merge with or can acquire. Yet, many of these merger and acquisition deals do not achieve the intended objectives. Companies that merge or acquire fail to create the right type of synergy for obtaining significant business growth or profits because of lack of cultural compatibility.

Companies are now focusing their efforts on cultural integration post the completion of merger or acquisition deal. However, culture plays an important role not only during merger or acquisition deals but also during the execution of daily operations in any organization. Company culture eventually plays a key role in shaping the narrative for the corporate brand.

Culture exists in every organization irrespective of whether the cultural code is explicitly articulated. Employees and new hires will behave in certain ways as per the written and unwritten rules of the company. Each organization's culture comprises of intentional and unintentional practices, language, norms and expectations. Culture shows the way things really work in an organization. Culture determines the expected behaviour that is required to succeed in an organization. Talent or employees are the primary sources of competitive advantage for any organization. Human resources in any company can innovate to create new products or services. Talented workforce in the marketing and sales functions can generate new business while employees in the operations function can ensure high level of customer satisfaction.

Employees can be the greatest advocates for the brands related to their organizations. Employees' passion for their products or services will rub off on the customers as well who in turn will begin to favour the brand over other competitors. We can observe this phenomenon among employees working for the customer support function. Customer support executives who have deep knowledge of company products or services can address queries quickly thereby leading to high customer satisfaction.

Companies need quality talent to execute corporate strategies and to achieve high business growth. Hence, companies must promote their corporate brands to attract good candidates. A corporate brand needs to focus on its organization culture to attract and to retain a quality workforce.

Organization culture can range from empowering and collaborative to hostile and toxic. When a candidate joins a company as an employee, he takes some time to orient himself with the company environment. Meanwhile, the preconscious mind of the candidate notes the various aspects of the company culture such as the overall cleanliness, facilities that are available for the employee such as cafeteria and restrooms, friendliness of co-workers and superiors, tone of language used in daily communication and so on.

The preconscious mind of any employee can quickly determine the unwritten rules or the real culture in any organization. The employee will soon be able to understand the "water cooler talk" in his organization.

Once an employee is able to understand the real culture in his organization, how does he react to it? The employee may find the culture to be compatible to his own values and hence he will feel comfortable and will be productive in the organization. The employee may also feel that the company culture is not compatible with his values and hence the employee may quit the organization soon. The company may have to pay an enormous cost if its culture is toxic to its employees.

The organization may spend lot of resources to hire and to train an employee but this employee may soon leave the company because of its hostile culture.

Employees who are disgruntled with a toxic company culture can adversely affect the corporate brand in two ways. These employees can leave the organization and can spread the word about the hostile work culture at their previous employer. These frustrated employees can also stay in the same organization and would work at a bare minimum level of productivity and motivation. Employees' lack of motivation will adversely affect the product or service quality levels. As a result, customers may not prefer to maintain their loyalty to a specific brand.

Leaders can shape the organization culture by clearly explaining and embracing the expected behaviours. The leadership team can have a well-defined vision, mission and values for the organization for consciously shaping the corporate culture.

Leaders can understand the organization culture by analysing the employee experience within the company. Corporate leaders can conduct employee engagement surveys or confidential focus groups to understand the various intricacies of organization culture.

Company leadership can understand what is working and what is not working within the corporate culture by using employee engagement or culture survey. The survey can use a combination of open and close-ended questions to understand the employee perception about company culture.

An employee focus group can enable the leadership to conduct a detailed analysis of the employee experience regarding company culture. An external consultant can facilitate such focus groups. Employees can be reassured about the confidentiality of focus group sessions. The facilitator can extract key ideas or themes from these discussions. These core ideas will highlight the various issue related to the company culture.

A dedicated team must collate and analyse the data obtained from culture surveys or employee focus groups. This team can provide recommendations or insights on improving various aspects of company culture.

Finally, company can focus on providing culture-specific training for managers and leaders. Learning programs related to corporate culture will impart the necessary behavioural skills to leaders and managers across the organization. Hence, companies can impart behavioural skills related training to their leaders and managers in order to foster the desired culture across the organization.

Company culture plays an important role in empowering and motivating employees. A motivated employee can act as a brand advocate to attract new customers. Empowered employees are more productive and can ensure to retain the brand loyalty of existing customers.

A company with toxic culture will comprise of disgruntled employees and individuals who like to play political games. Hostile work culture will soon reflect on an organization's products and services. Hence, company leadership must consciously shape the organization culture. An empowered corporate culture will transform the organization's employees into brand advocates.

CONCLUSION

Preconscious minds of consumers can detect brands and can learn the appropriate motor responses. These learned responses or muscle memories determine the customer loyalty towards any specific brand.

A coherent brand identity is crucial for grabbing the attention of any consumer. A brand also provides deeper meaning for its consumers with its identity. Consumers connect with brands not only at a transactional level but also at an emotional level.

A robust brand identity provides the essential emotional outcomes for the customers. Hence, a strong brand identity can be a source of huge strategic advantage to companies.

We can design a compelling brand identity or narrative using various levels of BrandChakra™ model such as social attraction, functional benefit, emotional trigger, sensory appeal and greater cause. We can analyse our product or service attributes as well as competitor brands to determine as to which levels of BrandChakra™ model we must apply for designing our brand identity.

Creating an interesting brand is both an art as well as science. Hence, we need to think from a holistic perspective to create a compelling brand identity.

I hope that this book provided you with some insights for designing unique marketing campaigns and brand identities. You can write to me at ramanathanj@outlook.com if you want to say hello or if you would like to share some interesting ideas. I wish you good luck as you progress further in your quest towards creating fascinating marketing campaigns and brands.

www.ingramcontent.com/pod-product-compliance
Lightning Source LLC
Chambersburg PA
CBHW030636220526
45463CB00004B/1544